C000193322

THE ROUTEMASTER

THE ROUTEMASTER

Michael H. C. Baker

Ian Allan
PUBLISHING

First published 2010

ISBN 978 0 7110 3541 6

Published by Ian Allan Publishing

an imprint of Ian Allan Publishing Ltd,
Hersham, Surrey, KT12 4RG

Printed in England by Ian Allan Printing Ltd,
Hersham, Surrey, KT12 4RG

Code: 1011/C2

Distributed in the United States of America and Canada by BookMasters Distribution Services

Visit the Ian Allan Publishing website at
www.ianallanpublishing.com

For James Henry Baker

Front cover: Designed specifically for London Transport, the Routemaster proved extraordinarily long-lived. Here RML2618 pauses at Hyde Park Corner on 19 March 2005, by which time it was 38 years old.
Matthew Wharmby

Back cover: Among 20 Routemasters retained for use on 'heritage' routes in Central London is RM1650, reprising the livery applied to 25 RMs in 1977 to celebrate HM The Queen's Silver Jubilee. It is seen away from its regular haunts, at Tower Hill, while participating in a running day on 17 September 2006.
Matthew Wharmby

Half title: The big event of 1983 was London Transport's Golden Jubilee. Included in this line-up at the Chiswick Works open day, held on the weekend on 2/3 July, are the first four Routemasters built.

Previous page: A pristine RM975, of Holloway garage, poses for London Transport's official photographer in Parliament Square in the spring of 1962.
London Transport Museum

Except where individually credited, all photographs are by the author or from the author's collection.

Contents

Introduction

To begin at the beginning. The Routemaster is a big, red, double-deck London bus. You probably knew that, but it's quite possible one big, red double-deck London bus looks much like any other to you. Unless you are an enthusiast. Or an anorak. Or Boris Johnson. Or Ken Livingstone; remember him? Don't let that bother you. By the time you have finished reading this book, or at any rate looking at the pictures, you will know precisely what distinguishes the Routemaster from all other London buses. Perhaps. I'm not banking on that, merely hoping. A couple of weeks ago I said to my wife: 'How about if we go up to Putney to take some photographs of RT1 and then we'll spent the rest of the day walking along beside the Thames?' My wife, Maeve, a headteacher and therefore well able to distinguish minute variations in pupils, parents, staff and which edicts from on high will still apply by the end of the week, has been married to me for 42 years and has attended countless bus rallies in that time, admittedly mostly fleetingly, either at the beginning or the end, but she has been there. So when the magnificent RT1, dating from 1939, beautifully restored and the subject of a

£150,000 appeal, to keep it in Britain at Cobham Bus Museum rather than let it go to Switzerland, a lot less than the cost of retaining a Titian (not a misprint for Titan) and, going by weight and volume, far better value, hove into view across Barnes Common and drew to a halt at the Putney Common terminus of route 22, just as it used to do in the 1940s and '50s, she enquired: 'Now is that a Routemaster?'

A few years back I was interviewed, at length, by a television company on the Routemaster, and when the programme appeared the opening shots depicted just about every bus which had ever been painted red, but none of them happened to be a Routemaster. It got better after that, but it wasn't a good start. Also the whole of my several hours of erudite chat about the Routemaster had disappeared and with it my chance of ever appearing with Julie Christie; such is show business.

The RT family of buses numbered almost 7,000, unique in the annals of public transport worldwide. It was under construction from 1938 to 1954, with a break during World War 2, and was the precursor of the Routemaster. The Routemaster first appeared in public in 1956, the intention being that the type should replace all the RTs, but it never did. Some 2,876 Routemasters were built, the last coming out in 1968. That was the year we were married, so you would think that would have had some resonance with Maeve, but seemingly not. You can see that you could hardly expect to replace nearly 7,000 buses with a mere 2,760, and in the pages that follow we will discover why more Routemasters were not built. Both the RT and the Routemaster came from London Transport's own design team, in co-operation with AEC, which for some 60 years provided the chassis and engines for the great majority of London's buses. Both were extraordinarily long-lived. Any bus which lasts 20 years, particularly with its original owner, can congratulate itself on a job well done. RTs served London for 40 years, although no actual individual bus was in service that long. The Routemaster did even better, not disappearing from ordinary service until 2005, and a handful still operate two 'heritage' routes. None of the buses still working in December 2005 was less than 37 years old, and some were more than 40. If that's not an icon, I don't know what is.

A line-up of RTs and Routemasters at Catford in 1973 which clearly reveals the differing front-end profiles of the two types.

The Concept 1

By 2005 the Routemaster had become one of the great legends – perhaps the greatest legend – of the bus world. Yet it was conceived very much as a compromise. Its predecessor, the RT, came into a world where bus travel was the norm for the population of London and the Home Counties, and although World War 2 interrupted its production to the extent that, after the first 151, five years and four months would pass before the next one took up service, the early postwar years were times of austerity, when private motoring was much restricted and bus travel was still just about for everyone. So whilst fuel economy and capacity were very important considerations – the RT was the first London mass-production bus to have the more economical diesel rather than petrol engine from the start – nevertheless paring down the weight and perhaps reducing comfort and interior appointments were not priorities. Even so, by the time RT production ended in 1954 the downturn in bus travel was beginning; watching television was becoming a popular, almost universal evening activity (although it would not be until the following year that ITV offered

an alternative to BBC), and more and more families owned a car, perhaps two, for young men – and, to a lesser extent, young women – still living at home might expect to own their first car, quite possibly a prewar Austin Seven, making them independent of public transport. In 1935, some two years before design work began on the RT, a wide-ranging traffic survey across England recorded an average of 11 vehicles passing each hour. By 1954 this figure had increased to 154. We are specifically not told, but it is fair to assume that the number of PSVs on the road would have been roughly the same each time.

In 1950 Green Line receipts fell by 6.6% compared with 1949, and throughout the decade this trend would continue. Bus receipts also fell, those in the Country Area reflecting the declining fortunes of the Green Line network, those in the Central Area rather less dramatically. London Transport had over-estimated its needs, and when the last RT rolled off the production line it and 80 others, all in Country Area green livery, plus 63 red examples of the RTL, the Leyland version, went straight into store. They gradually entered service, the last not until August 1959, each one replacing an older RT or RTL but certainly not one which would have been withdrawn in the normal course of events, and just about all would be sold, at bargain prices, continuing for many years with their new owners.

So the RT's replacement had to be more economical than the RT. It was wider by six inches and carried eight more passengers yet weighed no more. The Routemaster initially would be a replacement for London's trolleybuses, its fleet being the largest in the world, but when this had been accomplished it would continue in production and gradually take over the RT family's duties.

There was absolutely no doubt what RM stood for, and perhaps this was the very first designation of a London type about which this could be said without a shadow of a doubt. Several authors have made quite lucrative careers – or at least they would have done if anyone had been prepared to pay them – speculating on what RT actually meant, and although it seems fairly safe to assume that 'ST' stood for 'short type', 'STL' for 'short type lengthened', 'STD' for the Leyland version ... hang on, surely that should have been STL? No, of course that had already been used, so logic decreed the last letter of Leyland – but then why not the last letter of 'lengthened' for the long LT type? Logic then flies completely out of the windscreen with 'T' for the contemporary single-decker, which would have been all right if it had been a Leyland Tiger but was not exactly appropriate for an AEC Regal.

Not all names stick. The Routemaster's successor as the capital's standard double-decker, the DMS, was launched with a great flourish as the 'Londoner' – a name which might have been applied to anything or anyone from most of the bus's passengers to a culinary delicacy such as jellied eels and which, not surprisingly, proved about as popular as the Fire of London and, unlike that, failed to catch on. But as most Routemasters had the letters 'RM', either on their own or combined with

Preceding the Routemaster as London's standard double-decker was the RT-class AEC Regent III, and this type continued to be used for trolleybus replacement even after the first RMs had been delivered. As though welcoming in the new era, the sun shines on Sutton's RT191, seen beneath the now redundant wires in Wallington, on 4 March 1959.

others, applied in front of their number then it was inevitable that the name and the bus became synonymous. Initially the word Routemaster was also placed above the fleet number, although the *cognoscenti* assumed that this would disappear, like the cream upper-deck window surrounds on early RTs, on overhaul and were proved correct.

Did we think the Routemaster was as pretty as the RT? Not really. However, in one respect the former scored over the latter. People who know no better often use the description 'back of a bus' in a derogatory manner, but some buses have very shapely rears, and the Routemaster fell into this category. The back of the RT went straight up until making a sudden inward swing immediately below the upper-deck windows, but the Routemaster's rear curves were rather more subtle, beginning lower down at waist level and gradually increasing as they got higher.

The rear view changed little over the years (although platform doors were fitted to the coach versions) but the front took on various aspects. The very first official photograph came as a bit of a shock, not because it featured a 'tin front' rather than an exposed radiator, for such was all the rage in the mid-1950s and was to be expected, but it had a simple, single-piece destination display – very provincial and way below London standards. This was all part of the weight-paring exercise. The 'tin front' was a good deal better than that of many of its contemporaries, featuring the LT bullseye, some rather unnecessary chromium strips connecting it to the registration plate, which in the first photograph read 'LTE 1954', although, once sent out on the road this became SLT 56. Less than perfect visibility and problems with cooling soon prompted alterations. I first saw RM1 crossing Waterloo Bridge whilst working the 260 from Cricklewood garage in 1957 and thought the modified front, which incorporated a pronounced bulge, nothing short of ugly. The final, revised front as first featured on RM8 at the Commercial Motor Show in the autumn of 1958 was a vast improvement, and near-perfection was just about reached when this was modified to incorporate the traditional triangular AEC badge at the top.

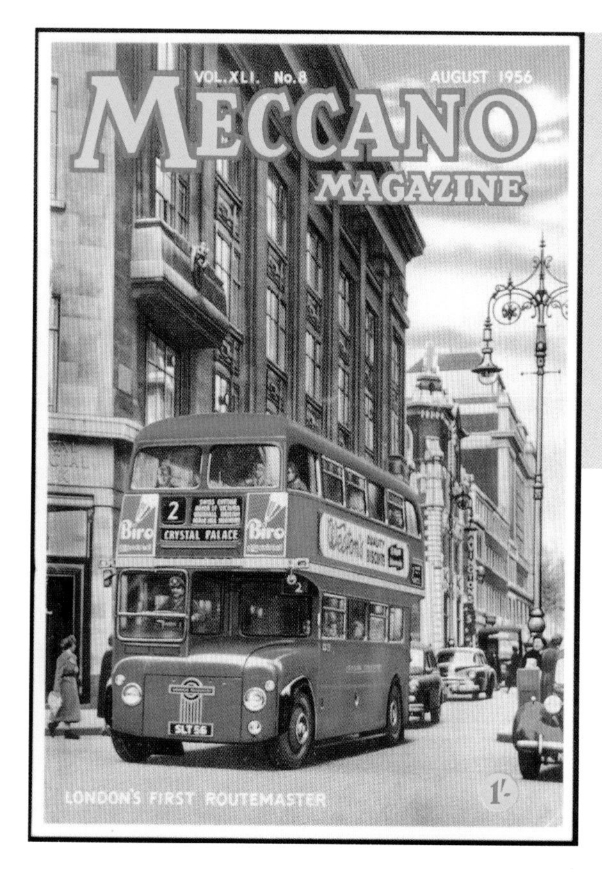

RM1 first appeared in public in 1954 with minimal destination apertures and 'LTE 1954' in place of registration plates. Although there was no AEC badge below the driver's cab this was displayed either side of the route indicator together with another for Park Royal Vehicles, which, of course, was as closely involved with the development of the Routemaster as was AEC. Not everyone liked the rather upright front end, especially noticeable when seen side-on, but which many considered actually rather well proportioned. Not surprisingly RM1 caused much interest; it was, after all, getting on for two decades since a new standard bus had appeared on the streets of London. The *Meccano Magazine* was still going strong in the mid-1950s and featured RM1 on its cover in August 1956.

Traditionally the lower side panels of London buses – indeed, just about all buses – had curved inwards, but not on the Routemaster, which as a result had a rather slab-sided appearance. Internally too it was not up to RT standards; I thought the combination of a distinctly lemon-yellowish roof panelling allied to a dominating maroon shade in the upholstery plus dark damask red window surrounds not particularly harmonious. Yet it was vastly better than much of what was happening out in the provinces, particularly the ghastly MCW Orion body, all on account of weight-saving as more and more passengers deserted public transport for private. Of course, beauty is in the eye of the beholder, handsome is as handsome does, etc, etc, and from a purely æsthetic point of view a half-cab design with a big hole above the bonnet and alongside the driver's cab can never match that of a bus or coach with a full front which can present a perfectly symmetrical aspect and would surely not offend Palladio.

The Routemaster had no chassis, this being replaced by two subframes, the main strength being provided by the aluminium-alloy body. Chassisless construction had been proved perfectly workable by the MCW 'L'-type trolleybuses, delivered in 1939/40 and destined to be the very last in service, being transferred around the system as the trolleybus network shrunk until taking part in the last rites from Fulwell depot early on 9 May 1962.

The Routemaster was never my favourite London bus; the STL and the RT could lay claim to elegance to which the Routemaster could never aspire. But the Routemaster possessed many virtues, not the least being that it has proved to be almost indestructible, giving the impression that it has always been there and always will be, a dependable, faithful old friend.

The Prototypes 2

It was hardly surprising that plans for the RT's successor were well underway before the last members of the family were delivered in 1954, for the RT was a design of the mid-1930s, and although in some respects it was *the* perfect London double-deck bus and would remain unsurpassed, had it not been for World War 2 production would probably have ended in the 1940s. Bus design had inevitably moved on, the Metropolitan Police (a pretty conservative body when it came to the regulation of public transport), had also moved on, and nationwide regulations permitted longer and wider vehicles. Looming on the horizon was the rear-engined bus upon which Leyland was working and which would be unveiled at the 1956 Commercial Motor Show as the Atlantean; this would utterly transform the double-decker but would be a step too far for London, at least for another generation.

There was no need to rush things, for the RT family, along with the RF class of AEC Regal IV single-deckers, had seen off all LT's prewar buses, and although the trolleybus fleet, the largest in the world, would need replacing by the late 1950s the vehicles

themselves were still, on the whole, in very serviceable condition. Just one prototype RT had been produced, and its predecessor, the STL, had

Considerably modified – particularly at the front end – since its first appearance and now working from Cricklewood garage on route 260, RM1 speeds across Waterloo Bridge on 4 May 1957.
London Transport Museum

gone straight into production, but in the period 1954-7 there appeared no fewer than four prototype Routemasters.

Extensive trials were conducted using all four prototypes, but in the summer of 1956, long before these had been completed (and with only RM1 in service) an order was placed for 850 production buses. The order went to AEC and Park Royal. No surprise there. Chiswick had long given up body production, concentrating on overhauls, and Park Royal, its factory just up the road from Chiswick, was, like AEC, a member of the Associated Commercial Vehicles group, whilst AEC was contracted to provide 75% of LT's bus production. However, it might have been thought that Weymann and Leyland, both large-scale suppliers of the RT family, would have been involved.

RM1 entered passenger service from Cricklewood garage on 8 February 1956, working initially on route 2 and later on the 260. Inevitably it had its teething problems; resolving these is, after all, the point of building prototypes. The seats were not up to RT standard and were soon replaced, but more significant development was the fitting later in 1956 of a new engine, of similar capacity as that used on the RT, but of monobloc construction. Known as the AV590, it would become the RM standard. Passenger service for RM1 ended in July 1959, it then becoming a trainer. In 1964 it was fitted with a standard RM front end which changed its appearance considerably.

A forlorn-looking RM1, although only the registration indicates this, sits in the dip on the test track in Chiswick Works on 28 July 1977. By 1973 it was no longer needed by London Transport and, despite its historic significance, had been sold to Lockheed Hydraulic Brake Co. It eventually returned to Chiswick, in effect dumped, as seen. Fortunately it was taken back by London Transport in 1980 and later joined the official London Transport Collection.

RM2 was completed at Chiswick in March 1956, looking virtually identical to RM1, but exhaustive tests followed, and it did not enter passenger service until May 1957. It was painted green and was put to work travelling between Redhill and Kingston on the 406; but not very often, there being problems with brakes and gearbox. August saw its last runs in the Country Area, whence it was taken back to Chiswick, painted red, and sent to Turnham Green where it could be seen working the 91. More experiments followed and its days in ordinary passenger service ended in November 1959. It then took up training duties, which lasted for some 13 years. *London Transport Museum*

EFE produced a rather nice model of RM2 in its short-lived Country Area green livery.

RM2 was painted green and after various trials and modifications entered service in May 1957 from Reigate garage on the 406. Its Country Area service was very brief, however, and much of that was spent of the road with gearbox and brake problems. Taken back to Chiswick in August that year, it was repainted red and sent down the road to Turnham Green garage, being used mainly on route 91. November 1959 saw it demoted to training work. Like RM1 it was later fitted with a standard RM front end.

The third Routemaster prototype, RML3, had a Leyland engine and a Weymann body, although it looked little different from RM1 and RM2. It took up passenger work on route 8 from Willesden garage in late January 1958 – six days after I completed National Service, as it happened,

RML3 was built not at Chiswick like its predecessors but by Weymann at its Addlestone factory, where production of RT bodywork had ended only two years earlier. The 'L' was on account of Leyland's supplying the engine and running units. There were various changes to the bodywork, inside and out, perhaps the most noticeable being a rather neater arrangement of the upper-deck front windows and a narrower bonnet lid, but that area was still rather a mess. After various false starts it went into passenger service from Willesden garage in January 1958 on route 8 and is seen here passing the Bank of England later that year. After a collision with a lorry in the Edgware Road in January 1959 it was repaired and thereafter was employed spasmodically in revenue-earning service, but by now its passenger-carrying days were almost over, and in November of that year it became a trainer.

although the two events were not linked. However, it did give me the chance, back employed as a trainee industrial photographer out and about in London and its suburbs, to get a picture of it passing the Bank. RML3 did even less front-line passenger service than its predecessors, like RM2 becoming a trainer in November 1959. With the advent of the 30ft-long Routemasters it was renumbered as RM3.

The last prototype was perhaps the most interesting, being a coach. It had a Leyland engine and, most interestingly, an ECW body. However, there was nothing in its appearance to suggest it was related to the Lodekka or any other ECW product, being very much of pure LT parentage, although, bearing in mind its intended use, much the most individual of the prototypes, with various refinements to fit it for life in Green Line service. Numbered CRL4, it was an impressive-looking vehicle with its electrically operated platform doors and attractive livery. Spacing was generous, seating – 32 up, 25 down – was more luxurious than on the bus version of the RM, and, if not a true luxury coach, this was certainly a very well-appointed bus. It began passenger duties in October 1957 from Romford garage alongside the RTs used on route 721 – essentially an express-bus operation. At the end of the year it was transferred to the much longer, cross-London 711 from Reigate to High Wycombe, which was otherwise, like most of the Green Line network, a single-deck RF preserve.

In August 1961 CRL4 was reclassified RMC4, 'L' henceforward being reserved for 30ft-long Routemasters, of which more anon. By this time its automatic transmission – hardly necessary on a vehicle not engaged in constant starting and stopping – had been replaced by a preselective, manually controlled system which was very similar to that which had served the RT so well. It moved around the garages, from Romford to High Wycombe, to Reigate, then to Tunbridge Wells for the 704, a garage which was something of an anachronism, being south and east of London Transport territory proper, operating only Green Line services, bus routes in the spa town being the province of Maidstone & District. Windsor garage

Perhaps the most interesting of all the prototypes was the fourth, CRL4, although it actually arrived before RML3. This was a coach, with an ECW body and Leyland engine and running units. ECW was not a major supplier to London Transport but it had previously built the bodies for the RFW coaches, which were the only true coaches in the London Transport fleet, and the GS normal-control, one-man single-deckers. CRL4, however, was pure Chiswick and was broadly similar to the three other prototypes, albeit with many modifications. It is pictured after delivery to Chiswick on 14 June 1957 and was the most handsome of the four in its Lincoln-green livery with pale-green window surrounds, polished front wheel trims and lamp surrounds and raised bullseye motif between decks. Internally it differed considerably from its predecessors and with green the predominant colour of the upholstery and side panels and cream ceilings was much the most attractive. The seats, 55 of them, had deeper cushions than those on the bus versions of the Routemaster. *London Transport Museum*

This view downstairs, looking towards the rear, shows the unusual single seats over the wheel-arches, which meant capacity was reduced from the original 57. There was also more room for luggage and parcels. Platform doors were fitted, and in every respect CRL4 represented a considerable improvement over the Green Line RTs, which were buses, pure and simple. It took up work, first of all on the 721 from Aldgate, which was worked by RTs, and was then tried out on various other routes. Amongst modifications were those made to the rear suspension and the restoration of the longitudinal seats, but it continued on Green Line and then Country Area bus work and, as far as is known, never worked as a training bus. *London Transport Museum*

also operated the 704, so RMC4 lived there for a while. Next it was up to the north east, to Harlow and Epping, then across to Stevenage, where it stayed until early 1963, by which time production RMCs were also allocated there. It was certainly a well-travelled vehicle, all the time being in passenger service, in contrast to the other three prototypes which, once production RMs were at work in the Central Area, were relegated to training duties, and we shall pick up its career in a later chapter.

All four prototypes would eventually be preserved.

The prototypes did not often have to cope with conditions like these, experienced by RML3 and RMC4 at Cobham in April 2008.

3 Trolleybus replacement

It was not until Stage 4 of trolleybus replacement, in November 1959, that Routemasters were used, partly because there were plenty of surplus RTs and RTLs available for the first three stages and partly because production of RMs was rather slow. It was the East End that first saw RMs *en masse*, although many were not actually brand-new, a number having been used since July on a trial basis at various garages which operated routes passing through Central London. By November 1959 there were 39 RMs either in passenger service or being used to train the drivers who were going to be converted from trolleybuses. In that month they all moved eastwards, joining others newly arrived there. Poplar depot was allocated 61, and West Ham 16, to replace trolleybus routes 567, 569 and 665.

I consulted the local papers to gauge the reaction of local people to the arrival of the new diesel buses. Despite searching diligently through the pages of the *East London Advertiser* of Friday 13 November 1959 – the changeover was on the night of 10/11 November – I could find absolutley nothing on the subject. Eventually, however, in the following week's edition, I found, buried deep on an inside page, a brief two-column report that 'passengers liked the interior heating system, and the extra space down the gangway', that 'conductors at West Ham Garage, Plaistow, like the buses' on account of 'the cubby hole under the stairs [through which] runs a hot-air pipe belonging to the heating system' and which 'conveniently dries off the busman's jackets which are stored there while on a run'.

The truth of the matter was that for the ordinary passenger the Routemaster was no big deal. The trolleybuses it replaced in the East End were amongst the most modern in the fleet, and rather than being scrapped most moved westwards, taking over from older vehicles. I had been an occasional user of the trolleybus, mostly our local 630, but

RM8, the first production Routemaster to be completed, seen at the 1958 Commercial Motor Show at Earl's Court. Particularly noticeable is the revised front end, far neater and better proportioned than anything hitherto seen on a Routemaster. *London Transport Museum*

as I now ventured further afield to explore the contracting network I was continually struck by how comfortable and up-to-date, if sometimes a little shabby, the London trolleybus fleet was. The abandonment of the trolleybus system was due to a number of factors, not least the increasing expense of maintaining its infrastructure, which dated back to tramway days. If we look back to the reaction of the

Why was the first production bus numbered RM8 rather than RM5, you might ask. Apparently RM5-7 were to have been test vehicles, but in the event they were standard buses, which RM8 never really was. Assembled by Park Royal ahead of the setting up of the production line, it was used for various experiments, spending no less than 18 years so employed, not entering passenger service until March 1976. It is seen that year, shyly peering around RM604 inside Sidcup garage Taking centre stage is RT1586.

press and the public in the 1930s as the trolleybus took over from the tram we can see how much greater was the impact. It wasn't until the war years that all the remaining trams were fitted with windscreens, and in the late 1930s one without such a basic facility, dating back to Edwardian times, compared very badly with a smooth-running, full enclosed, comfortably upholstered, almost silent trolleybus.

One of the greatest advantages of trolleybus abandonment, as far as London Transport and its customers were concerned, was that with the abolition of the 'unsightly' overhead power lines the authorities in Westminster and the City of London had no objection to former trolleybus routes' running right across London. Of course, motor-bus routes had done so since the earliest days, and now numerous former trolleybus and motor-bus routes could be amalgamated, extended and altered, to the benefit of all.

Routemaster production was now in full swing. By December 1959 the highest-numbered example in service was RM135. A year later the total, with eight stages of trolleybus replacement completed, had reached 500. Most of the East End had now lost its trolleybuses, and RMs now not only climbed the heights to Highgate Village, without needing (unlike the trolleybuses) any additional braking power, but also reached West Croydon and Uxbridge, respectively the southernmost and most westerly extremities of the erstwhile trolleybus network.

The year 1961 saw a spurt in Routemaster production, so that by December the total had reached almost 1,000, the newest, allocated to West Ham, being RM991, one of a batch which saw off the last trolleybuses from the East End. Routemasters had also replaced them in the far north-east, at Edmonton and Enfield, and the famous Aldgate terminus now was the exclusive preserve of the motor bus and coach.

Perhaps the most notable of the 1961 deliveries were 24 thirty-footers, placed in service in November from Finchley garage (hitherto a trolleybus depot) on route 104. After the first three had been delivered as ER880-2 the type classification was changed, the batch entering traffic as RML880-903. The extra

It was not until 11 November 1959 that Routemasters took up the work for which they had originally been intended, *i.e.* replacing trolleybuses. Sixty-one RMs went to Poplar and 16 to West Ham, where they replaced trolleybus routes 567, 569, and 665 with motor-bus routes 5, 5A, 48 and 238, whilst the existing route 23 also received some RMs. RM201 is seen on the forecourt of West Ham depot, which at that time was still operating trolleybuses, with none other than RM1 behind on training duties and giving us the chance to appreciate the much-improved front end of the production buses.

length was achieved by inserting an extra half-bay amidships and allowed an increase in seating capacity from 64 to 72. However, the remarkable thing was not that they were particularly revolutionary but that London Transport did not immediately switch to this length for all its future buses. But the truth is that London Transport, which under Lord Ashfield and Frank Pick had been the envy of big-city transport authorities the world over, was now timid, reactionary and beset by a combination of falling patronage and union disputes, and the next 30ft Routemasters would not appear until the spring of 1965.

Trolleybuses at Finchley, Stonebridge and Colindale just managed to last into 1962.

Two generations of 8ft-wide buses at Waterloo on 9 February 1960. Poplar RMs 29 and 128, working the 48, stand alongside two Hackney RTWs, 143 leading.

Neither the City of London nor Westminster cared much for overhead wires, and each did its best to keep out both the trams and the trolleybuses that succeeded them. The closest the latter got to the heart of the City was Finsbury Square – or Moorgate, as London Transport preferred to call it. The 641 would last until November 1961, although 'H1' trolleybus No 829, already the last of its type, would be gone before then. In this 5 April 1960 picture it is passing RM163 which had entered service, along with the 256, from Walthamstow on 3 February 1960. Behind is a Tottenham RTW on the 76.

The first Routemasters to reach the author's part of the world on scheduled duties arrived on 20 July 1960, which meant that London's longest all-day trolleybus route, the 630, had gone. Croydon was also the southernmost point reached by London's trolleybus network. The 630 had been based at Hammersmith, but the depot was in the way of the new flyover, and its space was also needed to house BEA coaches; fortunately there was room at Shepherd's Bush for the Routemasters. RM369 is seen at the West Croydon terminus of replacement route 220 on 20 July, the overhead wires not yet removed. Turning away is RM270 on route 64, which found itself involved in the trolleybus-replacement programme, being extended from West Croydon to Wimbledon Stadium. Two developments to the RM fleet will be noticed – the change from VLT to WLT registrations, which took place after RM300, and the fitting of opening windows at the front of the upper deck, this featureing introduced on RM254. Seven RMs were sent to Elmers End to supplement Croydon's RTs on the 64; RM270, its stint on the 64 over for the day, is heading home.

Highgate depot (nowadays Holloway garage) had been home to more trolleybuses than any other London, or indeed, British depot. February 1961 saw 117 Routemasters arrive to supplement a few that were already there, one being RM575, pictured in Highgate on its first day in service. The 517 had terminated at Holborn Circus but replacement route 17 was able to head through the City, over Blackfriars Bridge, and terminate at Camberwell Green. The 609 has not yet gone; Highgate played a part in this, but it was mostly the responsibility of Finchley depot, from which 'L3' No 1488 is working.

An oddball was RM664, which was turned out unpainted, in an attempt at cost-cutting, which had certainly proved successful on Underground trains – although they didn't look very pretty. RM664 did when brand-new, as in this official Chiswick picture taken in July 1961, but it did not wear well, and the experiment ended four years later when it painted red. *London Transport Museum*

By November 1961 the replacement of trolleybuses by new Routemasters was a regular occurrence, but the replacement of the 609 by the 104 was something else. Stretching the Routemaster to the recently legalised maximum length of 30ft enabled it accommodate 72 passengers, and 24 such vehicles, initially classified ER but soon changed to RML, were ordered and arrived in time to inaugurate route 104, which replaced the 609, worked by Finchley depot. RML884 is seen here in Finchley on its first day in service, 8 November, ahead of 'L3' trolleybus No 1449.

Their final day was 2 January, and what a day it was, with snow and slush on the main roads and, despite a weak sun managing to break through in the afternoon, many of the trolleys completing their final, rush-hour duties plastered with snow. Routemasters never took up residence at Colindale,

RML888 pops its head out of Finchley garage on the same day in the company of one of the former STL recovery vehicles and 'L3' No 1460, a trolleybus which had been working the 621, also replaced that day and which ought to have departed the previous evening but had, for some reason, refused to go.

but the large space behind the depot had been a trolleybus graveyard throughout the abandonment programme. One class which managed to escape was the postwar 'Q1', almost all its members being sold for further service in Spain.

The great London trolleybus network finally came to an end on the night of 8/9 May 1962 with the closure of Isleworth and Fulwell depots (the latter remaining open as a bus garage), which was where it had all begun back in LUT days. The splendid postwar 'Q1' trolleybuses, which had replaced the original LUT 'Diddlers', had left for a very different life in sunny Spain, their places taken by Leyland 'K1s' and 'K2s' and AEC 'L3s'. It was an area I knew well, for a regular family outing of ours involving extensive trolleybus participation had been to Hampton Court, which

The only way, short of a complete redesign, of lengthening the Routemaster by 2ft 6in was to insert an extra half-bay amidships. In theory this should not have improved the vehicle's handsome looks, but over the years the general consensus has been that it did no harm at all, as this picture of RML898, taken inside Stockwell garage in June 1965, surely conveys. *Ian Allan Library*

Dramatic conditions were encountered on 3 January 1962, when trolleybuses ceased running from Colindale and Stonebridge depots. The previous Sunday, 31 December, a remarkably heavy fall of snow had blanketed London and the Home Counties, causing considerable disruption to traffic, and although by Tuesday 2 January snow had been cleared from most of the main roads, services were still disrupted, the snow still clinging to the vehicles themselves and, in particular, covering the wide forecourt of Stonebridge depot. 'N1s' and 'N2s', transferred across from East London, perform their last duties on 2 January. The RT has many more years of service left.

A pair of Routemasters, RM971 leading, arrive at Stonebridge on 2 January 1962, ready to take up work the following morning.

Colindale depot never became a bus garage but it still had a melancholy service to perform, that of breaking up most of London's trolleybuses. The very last prewar design was the 'P1', which did not actually take up work until the early war years. No 1716, still largely intact, awaits its fate at the back of Colindale depot on a miserable day in January 1962.

meant boarding a 630 where the Purley Way met Stafford Road, just short of Mitcham Common, an extensive tour of the south-western suburbs of Mitcham, Tooting, Earlsfield, Wandsworth, over the Thames at Putney, and so to Hammersmith, where we changed onto a 667 which would take us past Chiswick Works and glimpses of all sorts of wonders within, through Brentford, Isleworth and Twickenham to our destination. One of the glimpses, in the early days during the war and just after, had been of the 'Diddlers' in and around Hammersmith, which with their upright aspect and clumsy front end looked to me like something left over from another age compared with the elegant and still modern-looking standard London trolleybus, whether of the pre- or postwar variety. Had I been told that they were close relations of the 'Feltham' tram (just about my favourite means of transport once I had quit my cerulean blue pushchair), emanating from the same design team (the 'Felthams', not my pushchair, at least as far as I know), I would have simply dismissed this as yet another fairy tale from my then – sorry, but it's true – favourite author, Enid Blyton. A number of

On the last day of trolleybus operation 'Diddler' No 1, in far-from-pristine condition, having been preserved in the condition in which it was withdrawn from regular service in 1948, poses alongside RM1127 on the forecourt of Fulwell depot. Note the tram tracks; this was one of several locations where these could still be seen and, indeed, would remain for many years to come. *London Transport Museum*

Various alterations were made to the former Kingston trolleybus routes to make them less self-contained. The new 285 connected New Malden with Heathrow Airport, and RM1123 has just crossed Kingston Bridge and is seen heading through Hampton Wick in the summer of 1962. *Ian Allan Library*

commemorative runs were made on the last day, the most notable by the preserved original 'Diddler', No 1, which was towed from its then resting place and allowed just one run, being in such a fragile state that there was much trepidation as to whether even this was asking too much of it. The very last trolleybus in service, 'L3' No 1521, now resides in contented and still active retirement beside the sea – well, pretty close to it – at the East Anglia Transport Museum at Carlton Colville, near Lowestoft, along with several other trolleys and a London tram.

As with every abandonment, various alterations were made to what had been trolleybus routes, emphasising one of the principal reasons why the trolleybus, with its inability to venture from beneath its overhead power source had to go. The new 285 route connected New Malden and Kingston with Heathrow Airport, a very useful link; one would not have liked to see the undercarriage of a low-flying Vickers Viscount become entangled with the trolleybus overhead. Nevertheless, Kingston was that much less of a transport enthusiast's Mecca after 9 May 1962.

RM1000, placed in service the spring of 1962, received a unique registration sequence, as apparent from this 1970s photograph taken at Broad Green, Croydon. Happily the pedestrian made it across the road unscathed!

4 Replacing the RT family

Completion of the trolleybus-replacement programme certainly did not signal the end of Routemaster production, for the intention was that the type should eventually replace the entire RT family. Because of its slightly greater capacity London Transport had hoped to replace every 10 RTs with nine RMs, but the unions would have none of it. So when the first post-trolleybus-era RT-family replacement took effect in December 1962 an equal number of RMs replaced the RTLs which had been working the 73 from Tottenham and Mortlake garages, followed by Routemasters on two other long-established Central London routes, the 13 and the 16. The RTL, never as popular with drivers as the RT, began to head towards extinction, 141 having been withdrawn by the end of 1962. However, proving that Leyland engines were not entirely out of favour, some 574 RMs so equipped would be delivered in the period 1962-4.

Once the trolleybuses had gone attention turned to the RT family, the Leyland-engined versions generally being withdrawn first. In this view at Victoria, recorded in June 1964, an RTW (left) is working route 76, RM1692 the 16 (which 18 months previously had lost its RTLs), and RTL633 the 52, with roofbox RTL68 alongside on the 32.
David Smithies

Many Routemaster deliveries in the early 1960s were fitted with a Leyland engine in place of the a standard AEC unit. Among these was RM1332, seen heading through Barking in the spring of 1979.

The use of the letters 'LT' in the registration – a nice touch – had come to an end with the appearance of RM1601 (601 DYE). RM1651, of Riverside garage, faces up to a sudden snowstorm in Sloane Street in January 1973.

5 Forward-entrance Routemasters

I've more than once referred to the notion that by the beginning of the 1960s, if not before, the Routemaster concept was distinctly dated. Front-entrance double-deckers, on which the driver could monitor passengers as the boarded and alighted (and ultimately take fares, thereby saving operators the conductor's wages) were becoming the norm. As yet AEC had not developed a rear-engined double-decker to rival the Leyland Atlantean or the Daimler Fleetline, so it was perhaps not surprising that the highly flexible modular design of the Routemaster was adapted to produced a 30ft-long, 69-seat, forward-entrance bus. Unveiled at the 1962 Commercial Motor Show, it was then sent off to see if anyone else would like to buy this form of Routemaster. At this time I was a student at Liverpool Art College, and one afternoon I was standing at the 27 (Shiel Road Circular) stop near Wavertree when what should turn up but RMF1254. At that time I was more concerned with trying to persuade the youth of the city to take an interest in fine art rather than pop music, which we all knew would get you nowhere (although a number of my contemporaries had a friend, John Lennon, who was in a group called the Beatles, which, they assured us, was about to make the breakthrough into the big time). I didn't even know there was such a thing as a forward-entrance Routemaster, let alone that it would be sent on an autumn sabbatical beside the Mersey. Anyhow, I climbed aboard and reflected on what an improvement it was over the Corporation's standard fare, on which seats were seemingly provided only with a good deal of reluctance. In the end the Corporation said 'No thanks' and sent it back to London, preferring to invest in a fleet of rather well-appointed Atlanteans.

RMF1254 never did enter service with London Transport (more trade-union resistance) and was eventually sold to Northern General, far away in the North East. Northern General was the only operator outside London to buy new Routemasters. Eighteen forward-entrance examples, broadly similar to RMF1254 but with Leyland engines, had been delivered in the spring of 1964, to be followed by a further 32 later in the year and early 1965.

Northern General 2086, one of that company's first batch of 18 Routemasters, pictured at AEC's Southall works prior to delivery in the spring of 1964.

If the forward-entrance Routemaster failed to find a welcome with London Transport it nevertheless became a familiar sight in West London, for British European Airways decided, having tried out RMF1254, to order 65 to work between its Gloucester Road air terminal and Heathrow Airport. The Routemasters replaced the 4RF4 1½-deck coaches, having 56 seats against the latter's 37. There would have been more had 30ft-long buses been ordered, but the shorter version was preferred so that

Trade-union objections ensured that forward-entrance RMF1254 never entered service with London Transport. After use by AEC as a demonstrator, during which time it was loaned to East Kent, Liverpool and Halifax and finally British European Airways, it was sold in 1966 to Northern General, joining 50 similar buses bought new in 1964/5. Pictured in Newcastle in August 1979, it would finally see normal service in London on 28 October 2005 (by which time London Transport had ceased to exist), being used to mark the end of Routemaster operation on route 38.

Of the 65 forward-entrance Routemasters delivered to BEA in 1965/6 most ultimately received British Airways' livery of blue and white. So adorned, NMY 628E is pictured at the West London Air Terminal in Gloucester Road in 1979, shortly before sale to London Transport.

a luggage trailer could be towed and remain within length regulations. They were capable of reaching 70mph although officially restricted to 50mph. They were maintained by London Transport engineers. Delivered in an attractive livery of blue and white separated by a black waistband, they later donned an altogether more garish orange and white, and later still, following BEA's merger with BOAC, most received British Airways blue and white. By 1975, however, 13 were deemed surplus to requirements, and these were purchased by London Transport, which, having carried out various modifications to render them suitable for stage-carriage work as the RMA class, placed them in service from Romford garage on route 175. Trade-union opposition (this time because of the lack of grab-rails) saw them withdrawn after less than a year, but this did not deter LT from snapping up the rest of the type as they were released by BA, most serving as staff buses and thereby releasing RTs and RMs for passenger service. Disposal of the RMAs began in the mid-1980s, but six would see further service in London on sightseeing work, and a number of others survive today in various uses, both in the UK and overseas.

Scheduled withdrawal of Northern General Routemasters began in 1978 and was completed two years later. A number eventually found their way to London. Two, although sent to Wombwell Diesels in Barnsley for breaking in 1978, did get to the capital in a manner of speaking as salvageable parts, whilst 12 more complete buses were bought by London Transport, and some appeared on sightseeing-tour duties. RMF1254 also came back south and is nowadays privately preserved. Several examples of other former Northern General Routemasters also survive, three of them in preservation.

Following acquisition by London Transport most of the former BEA Routemasters were put to work as staff buses. Still in British Airways livery, RMA51 is pictured alongside Metrobus M83 at the entrance to Fulwell garage in the summer of 1979.

In 1975 British Airways decided to dispose of 13 of its Routemasters and, with its rear-engined vehicles falling by the wayside in unmanageable numbers and British Leyland unable to supply sufficient spare parts for the otherwise dependable Routemasters, London Transport bought them and put them into service on the 175 at North Street garage, some still wearing the fairly repulsive orange livery applied latterly by BEA. Their use was very much a stop-gap measure, and the RMAs, as they became, found more permanent employment as staff buses or driver trainers. One of the latter, RMA5, is pictured at King's Cross in 1977.

6 Green Line

RMC4 was deemed to have been a success, Green Line passengers particularly appreciating the view from the upper deck, so in 1961 a batch of 68 production versions was ordered, these materialising in 1962/3 as RMC1453-1520. Patrons of routes 715, 715A, 716, 716A, 718, 719, 720 and 720A were the lucky ones who got to ride these fine vehicles initially.

Sadly Green Line patronage was declining steadily, something the double-deckers were unable to halt, and they were soon transferred between routes. At the end of 1964 the 720A reverted to RF operation, the RMCs displaced moving to the 717. However, London Transport felt there was still a niche for double-deck coaches, ordering 43 longer Routemasters, which entered service in 1965 as RCL2218-60. Weighing 8 tons unladen, which necessitated the fitting of an 11.3-litre engine, these seated 65 passengers and were intended to take over from the 15-year-old, 56-seat RTs working from Romford and Grays on the still heavily patronised East London routes which terminated at Aldgate. These, if only because of their greater length, were even more impressive than the RMCs. However, their careers as coaches would be severely curtailed; scarcely had the they entered service than London Transport had determined that the only way to stem losses on Green Line services was to convert them to one-person operation as soon as possible, and in 1969 12 RMCs were taken off Green Line work and sent to Hatfield and Addlestone garages for bus work.

In January 1970 London Transport's Country Area services, including the Green Line network, became the responsibility of a newly formed subsidiary of the National Bus Company, London Country Bus Services Ltd. In the early London Country days Aldenham continued to carry out overhauls, and when in 1971/2 the turn came for the RCLs there was little change to livery. However, the completion of the RCL overhaul cycle – the RMCs having already been dealt with in LT days – pretty well coincided with the end of Routemaster operation on Green Line

Turning out of Baker Street in the Marylebone Road RMC1470 illustrates what an impressive looking vehicles the Green Line 'coaches' were, with their electrically operated platform doors and attractive livery. Double headlights were a rather impressive feature that was in vogue on commercial vehicles and certain cars of the period.

The spring and early summer of 1965 witnessed the arrival of a further 43 Routemasters for Green Line work, these being the first 30ft examples since the original batch of Central Area buses, delivered four years previously. By now the property of London Country, RCL2234 is seen in 1970 at that traditional haunt of the Green Line double-decker, Aldgate, in company with London Transport 'Merlin' (AEC Swift) MBS171.

duties. Ninety AEC Reliance coaches – not that Reliance was a particularly apt a title for these not very reliable vehicles – entered service in 1971/2 and, being one-person-operated, replaced practically all the double-deckers. Like all Green Line vehicles, the Routemaster coaches had always done a certain amount of bus work, notably early in the morning when heading out from their garages to the country termini of their respective Green Line routes and they could usefully be employed operating on the bus route(s) which the Green Line route paralleled. By the late spring of 1972 RMCs and RCLs were operating (or had already operated) as buses from Romford, Reigate, Dorking, Dartford, St Albans, Hemel Hempstead, Hertford, Grays, Swanley and Guildford garages. The Green Line fleetname was replaced by 'London Country', and the light-green waistband by one in bright yellow which did not go particularly well with the dark (and often now rather shabby) Lincoln green. However, the application from 1973 of NBC leaf green to RMCs and RCLs brightened things up considerably.

Its journey from Tilbury to Aldgate almost complete, RCL2236 heads along the Commercial Road in 1970.

Uniquely just one Routemaster coach received full NBC livery with Green Line fleetname. This was RCL2237, which was repainted at Leatherhead in March 1975 and allocated to Godstone, where it served as a spare vehicle for the 709. When not so employed it worked as a bus from Crawley but is seen here, just after its repainting, at Chelsham in the company of a Leyland National coach (well that's how London Country described it even if the fare-paying passengers thought otherwise) and an RT.

On 1 January 1970 control of what had hitherto been London Transport's Country Area passed to London Country Bus Services Ltd, a newly formed subsidiary of the National Bus Company. Already some of the RMCs had been demoted to bus work, and within the next few years OPO on both coach and bus routes would become the rule; there would be no role for the Routemaster, in any of its forms. With a Merlin for company, RMC1455 is seen working the 330 in St Albans in 1973.

Just one regular Green Line duty remained, that on the 709, and as late as 1975 Godstone-based RCL2237 was uniquely repainted in full NBC livery, complete with double-arrow insignia and also Green Line fleetname to work rush-hour journeys from Godstone to London and back. This came to an end on 15 May 1976, when Leyland Nationals, laughably referred to as coaches, took over.

A remarkable survivor was RMC4, the passenger-carrying career of which had outlasted many times over those of the other three prototypes. As London Country retired its newer Routemasters in the late 1970s it remained in service, ultimately becoming the very last example operating from Hatfield garage. Finally withdrawn from normal service on 1 May 1979, it was retained for special events, the most significant being the Green Line Golden Jubilee in July 1980, for which it was restored to its original Green Line livery. RMC4 is now privately preserved and is often seen at rallies and on running days.

Many Routemasters lasted long enough with London Country to be repainted in NBC leaf green, complete with the NBC double-arrow symbol, which at least suited them better than the increasingly tired, dull-looking, often patched Lincoln green. In this photograph, taken in May 1977, RCL2240 of Chelsham has been repainted, whereas RCL2246, still proclaiming allegiance to its former home of Grays, retains the darker shade.

Remarkably RMC4, was still in service in 1978, long after the other three prototypes had been withdrawn from passenger duties. It is seen here inside Hatfield garage, looking for all the world like a standard member of the class. Withdrawn in 1979 and subsequently restored to its original livery for the Green Line 50th-anniversary celebrations in 1980, it has since become a regular on the rally circuit.

7 Rear-engined rivals

Immediately after the RCLs came 30ft-long RML buses, 500 being ordered for Central and Country Area use. They perpetuated the CUV…C registrations allocated to the last of the RMs and the RCLs and were all but identical to the original Finchley thirty-footers. These were the first bus versions of the Routemaster to be delivered to the Country Area, although MMCs and RCLs had often performed Country Area bus duties in true Green Line fashion. In October 1966 the first of 100 green-painted RMLs, RML2306, was delivered, to East Grinstead, others going to Godstone and Reigate garages, where they displaced RTs from the 409 and 411 routes. Godstone and East Grinstead had always kept their RTs in immaculate condition and, for a time, this tradition was maintained with their successors.

By this time the various teething troubles which had inevitably afflicted Routemasters in their early years had been eliminated, and the type was proving immensely reliable. It was, however, old-fashioned, and London Transport felt compelled to dip its foot into the rear-engined, off-the-peg double-deck world, and at the same time as it ordered the final 500 Routemasters it purchased 50 Atlanteans with

Among the 500 RMLs delivered in the years 1965-8 were 100 green-painted examples for Country Area bus routes. The first of these, delivered in October 1966, were allocated to East Grinstead garage, others going to Godstone and Reigate, where they displaced RTs from routes 409 and 411. Here, in February 1968, an RML has become stranded in Limpsfield High Street whilst working the 410 from Reigate to Bromley. Having recorded the scene the photographer, along with his father, helped to dig the bus out, enabling it continue its journey up the High Street before turning left along the A25 to Limpsfield Chart, thereafter crossing the Kent border to reach Westerham and, hopefully, climbing north-eastwards to Biggin Hill and on to its destination. *Ray Stenning*

Initially there were insufficient green Routemasters to replace all the RTs, so 17 red ones were sent to Godstone. One such was RML2299, seen here at West Croydon bus station, already looking rather work-stained, in October 1965. By the end of November all the red RMLs were able to depart for the Central Area.

bodies built, like those of the Routemasters, by Park Royal. But there the resemblance ended. Their interiors fell far short of the standard Londoners had come to expect, externally they were ill-proportioned, mechanically they were unreliable, and they were less economical than a Routemaster. Just about the only concession to service in London was the fitting of a three-piece destination indicator. So why on earth was the concept not dismissed out of hand? Essentially, if the mechanical problems could be overcome and it could be made somewhat more economical to run, the rear-engined bus, manned by the driver who could also collect the fares, was seen as the way forward if London, like the rest of the UK, was to come to terms with falling passenger numbers. The XAs, as the Atlanteans were classified, were put to work on the 24, one of the busiest Central London routes.

London Transport also bought eight Daimler Fleetlines (XFs), with bodies similar to the XAs' but painted green in anticipation of their use in the Country Area. These proved to be rather more successful. However, a far more exciting prospect was in hand. AEC had made a serious mistake in clinging for far too long to the half-cab layout, losing out to Leyland and Daimler (and even Guy), and London Transport had fallen into the same trap. In 1964 work had begun on a rear-engined Routemaster, and FRM1 (the 'F' signifying a front entrance) duly entered service in 1967. It shared 60% of its parts with the conventional Routemaster – a fact that was obvious from the plethora of windows, which gave it a rather dated appearance. Internally its origins were even more obvious. In many respects, however, it was a superb vehicle. It was

London's first Leyland Atlanteans were allocated to Chalk Farm garage and set to work on the 24, one of the busiest Central London routes. Seen at Trafalgar Square when new in the summer of 1965 is XA10, in the company of an RTW on the 11 and, hastily making its exit stage left, an RM on the 15.

comfortable, far better appointed than the XAs or XFs, and rode and handled superbly. For the best part of two years it worked in Central London on the 34B and 76 routes, although, inevitably, it often had to be sent back to Chiswick for attention. I got to know it well, for in December 1969 it moved to Croydon garage (now also home to the XAs) and took up work on the one-man-operated 233 between West Croydon and Roundshaw – a rather featureless housing estate but one with a fascinating history, having been built on the site of the old Croydon Airport, where British commercial aviation history had been pioneered in the 1920s and '30s. Sadly, like Croydon Airport, the world had moved on and away, and the FRM never went into production, it proving more cost-effective to buy off-the-peg 'provincial'-type buses.

The sole rear-engined Routemaster, FRM1, entered service in 1967 from Tottenham garage alongside Atlanteans on route 76 but in 1969 was reallocated to Croydon, being seen early in 1970 at the Roundshaw terminus of the 233 – another route shared with Atlanteans.

A rear view of FRM1 near Purley Way, Croydon. Transferred again, this time to Potters Bar, in 1973, it was to see out its career working from Stockwell and, finally, Victoria, on the Round London Sightseeing Tour, being eventually withdrawn in February 1983.

8 Production ends

In 1966 London Transport had published its now famous (or do I mean infamous?) report 'Reshaping London's Buses', wherein it declared its plans for the future. To stem increasing losses it envisaged a wholesale conversation to one-man operation (as it was then known), using high-capacity single-deckers, one-person operation of double-deckers having not yet been legalised. The Routemaster thus found itself out of favour, and production came to an end early in 1968 with completion of the order for 500 RMLs, delivery of which had commenced three years earlier. Most of the final batch were allocated to Croydon (TC) for use on the 130 group of routes, which connected Croydon with New Addington, although the very last, RML2760, went to Upton Park.

The Routemaster had not only failed to replace all the RTs – indeed, there were still more members of the RT family on London Transport's books than all the Routemasters put together (although the RTWs had gone, and RTLs would not last much longer) – but its successor was by the end of the year already at work. This was not, as yet, either the Daimler Fleetline or the Leyland Atlantean but a entirely different sort of bus, the single-deck, one-person-operated AEC Merlin. The half-cab, front-engined double-decker seemed to belong in the past, not only in London but throughout the UK, and the chances of the Routemaster's achieving anything like the lifespan of the RT class, which by 1970 was a more than respectable 31 years, seemed a pipe-dream. And yet, had we but known it, the Routemaster story was barely out of its infancy.

Routemaster production came to an end at the beginning of 1968. Croydon garage was scheduled to receive almost all of the final batch for use on the 130 group of routes, serving New Addington. In this view inside Croydon garage RML2758, two away from the very last Routemaster, is one of two roses next to a thorn, the latter being Atlantean XA12, the other rose RT2036. An estate planted atop the North Downs in the late 1930s but greatly expanded after the war, New Addington had always suffered from poor public-transport links, and the problem was never satisfactorily solved until the advent of Tramlink.

The very last Routemaster, RML2760, was sent not to Croydon but to Upton Park, where it entered service on 1 March 1968 and remained for decades, mostly working the 15, well into the 21st century – surely sort of record. It is seen here inside the garage in October 1991.

Uncertain times 9

Although red Routemasters remained well maintained through the early 1970s their future appeared little brighter than that of their country cousins. London Transport, by now under the control of the Greater London Council, was aiming to achieve 100% one-person operation by the end of 1978 – which would, of course, have meant no more Routemasters. The last of 650 AEC Swifts (which London Transport insisted were 'Merlins') delivered since early 1968 was placed service in October 1969, to be followed by the first of 700 shorter Swifts. However, it soon became clear that single-deckers were not the complete answer in London, for their capacity was simply insufficient. The buses themselves compounded the problem, for they proved to be nothing short of disastrous. Good-looking but mechanically unreliable and structurally suspect, they destroyed almost overnight the case for high-capacity, one-person-operated single-deckers in London.

Meanwhile London Transport, Daimler and Park Royal had been working on a rear-engined double-decker, and the result was displayed at the Commercial Motor Show in 1970. As had been the case

By the time the last Routemasters entered service early in 1968 the type's half-cab, open-platform layout was something of an anachronism, and the future was deemed to lie in the hands of high-capacity single-deckers such as the 36ft AEC Swift or, in London parlance, 'Merlin'. Ten years on, however, opinions had altered somewhat, and the only Merlins still in service were those employed on Red Arrow services. Illustrating the point is this view of an MBA and two Routemasters, RM836 nearer the camera, in Oxford Street in February 1979.

15 years earlier with the Routemaster, huge batches were ordered before the first deliveries had had a chance to prove themselves in service. Early examples had Gardner engines, but most of the later buses were Leyland-powered, while construction of the bodywork was shared by MCW. However, the DMS proved hardly more successful in service than the Swifts, although a good deal of the fault also lay with London Transport at various levels, not least with engineers who were wedded to practices which were

RM971 was the first to sport what is still a particularly colourful feature of the London bus scene, the all-over advertisement. Certainly bright red is the proper colour for a London bus, but exceptions provide a nice contrast, and although not all the advertisements have been an æsthetic success, that for Yellow Pages certainly was, establishing the rule that the brighter the main colour the better. Appearing in August 1969, not surprisingly on the 11, London's most famous route, RM971 is seen at Aldwych, keeping company with other Routemasters, Merlins and an RT.

The Daimler Fleetlines that followed the Swifts were scarcely any more successful, and most were withdrawn prematurely. DMS1, one of two that been exhibited at Earl's Court in 1970, had a longer life than most and upon its retirement in 1984 joined the London Transport Museum's collection. Since then it has appeared at various rallies, being seen here at the Science Museum's store at Wroughton airfield, on the downs above Swindon.

Representing three generations of London Transport double-decker at West Croydon in 1974 are RT1048 (centre), RCL2253 (both by now in London Country ownership) and DMS501.

fine for an era now gone but who seemed unable to adapt to that in which they now found themselves. It began to look as if there might be a future, certainly in the short term, not just for the Routemaster but also for the RT. Various members of the latter class began to reappear in Central London, helping out Routemasters, although often they were not in very good condition and were a sad contrast with their halcyon days.

On a more cheerful note 1977 was the year of the Queen's Silver Jubilee, and to celebrate this 25 RMs were decked out most fetchingly in a livery of

In the mid-1970s examples of the RT class reappeared in passenger service in Central London. Seemingly in reasonable condition, apart from a few roof dents and diesel stains below the filler cap, and with displaying a full set of blinds (not always the case), RT3949 stands on the forecourt of Walworth garage on 25 July 1977. Route 12 had been an RM exclusive for several years, worked by such vehicles as RM2204, which, with the RT, provides a neat sandwich for DMS161.

Elsewhere RTs was still officially allocated to some suburban routes. They lasted, for instance, at Palmers Green until February 1978 on the 261, and RT219, nominally one of the very earliest and thus some 30 years old, is seen here caught just before withdrawal in bright, low winter sun in the company of RMs 557, 627 and 192.

The 54 was still worked by Catford's RTs, three of which, among them RT2292 and RT1088, are seen here in April 1978 at the Fairfield Halls terminus in Croydon, just before being replaced by DMSs, as a Chelsham RMC working the 403 heads in the opposite direction.

all-over silver and temporarily renumbered SRM1-25. Costs were borne by advertisers, who could promote their products both inside and out. A touch of luxury was provided by the carpets, fitted on both decks, supplied at no cost to LT by the International Wool Secretariat (which sounds as if it should have had its headquarters in the Kremlin, but I don't think it did) to test the durability of its product. The SRMs were put to work both on routes serving Central London and some which were purely suburban, the

To mark HM the Queen's Silver Jubilee in 1977 25 RMs dating from the mid-1960s were outshopped in all-over silver livery and temporarily renumbered SRM1-25. Seen outside Grants department store in North End, Croydon, is SRM15 (better known as RM1903), sponsored by JVC. In 1964 Routemasters of this batch, commencing with RM1866 (ALD 866B), had introduced registration suffixes on London double-deckers.

Sponsored by Selfridges, SRM21 (otherwise RM1870) negotiates Hyde Park Corner while working route 7.

idea being that the silver buses would be seen far and wide, which would please the advertisers and also the general travelling public.

Meanwhile London Country, hell-bent on achieving 100% OPO as soon as possible, was laying aside its Routemasters and was coming to an arrangement with a certain yard in Yorkshire which would have seen the whole rapidly consigned to scrap. London Transport, in the nick of time realising the fate about to befall a fleet of buses which it regarded as a possible asset, stepped in and bought as many as it could. London Country had already written off 38 Routemasters, but London Transport decided that it could put 19 of these back on the road at a price less than purchasing a similar number of new buses, which would quite possibly would in any case have been less reliable than a fully overhauled

A picture illustrating the extent to which the magnificent RMLs were allowed to deteriorate following transfer to London Country. Only nine years old but looking very sorry for itself, RML2324 stands at the back of Godstone garage in 1975 in the company of RML2306 and a pair of Leyland PD3s acquired from Ribble (Burlingham-bodied driver trainer LR3) and Southdown (Northern Counties 'Queen Mary' LS3), the latter as a stop-gap measure to supplement the flagging Routemasters on routes 409 and 411.

Routemaster; parts were salvaged from the remainder. The RMLs were the most prized of all and were quickly given a complete overhaul at Aldenham, their transmission altered from semi- to fully automatic, and in May 1978 the first of the returning exiles began work in Central London, being quite indistinguishable from their always-red brethren. The RMCs which passed to London Transport took up work as trainers. There was no great urgency in repainting these, and although they quickly acquired the London roundel some retained their green livery for several years.

The very last passenger duties of London Country's Routemasters were at Chelsham and Swanley garages, RMC1512, based at the latter, working the final turn, on the 477 on 5 March 1979. The next

London Country had also found itself burdened with Merlins and was as frustrated by them as was London Transport. Their successor was the Leyland National; although much better this was not an unqualified success, but London Country eventually owned more than any other concern in the world. Meanwhile RTs and Routemasters were being laid aside, dumped at the back of various garages dotted around the Home Counties. RML2450, reduced to training duties, stripped of blinds and with a badly dented roof, stands miserably beside a Leyland National at Stevenage in 1978 with a less than complete RF in the distance.

The 403 was one of the very last strongholds of the London Country Routemasters. The great surprise of 1977 in the London Country world was the repainting in NBC green of three RTs, and their allocation to Chelsham to work the 403 and the 453 routes along with the RMCs and the RCLs. Seen here in the summer of 1977 are RT1018 and RT604 with, between them, RCL2240, all looking distinctly pleased with themselves in their bright-green colours.

day all London Country's remaining Routemasters – apart from RMC4 – became London Transport property. The RCLs had, like the rest, ended their days as buses, and London Transport decided that most of them were fit for similar work in Central London. To this end various modifications were carried out, most notably the removal of the doors and luggage racks and the fitting of stanchions and grab-rails, but the deep Green Line seat cushions were retained, making these just about the most comfortable buses in the entire fleet. All but three were so treated and sent to Stamford Hill and Edmonton garages, from where they worked on routes 149 and 279 into the City and West End, where they were much appreciated.

The express 403 continued to be worked by Routemasters until the first few days of 1980, when Leyland Atlanteans took over. RMC1501 is seen at West Croydon in December 1979, in company with Atlantean AN46 on the 408.

It was not in the least surprising that London Transport, having bought Routemasters from British Airways, should want to acquire many more from London Country, and it began to do so in December 1977. Some were in a deplorable condition, fit, one would have thought, only for scrap (which fate did indeed befall a handful), but so desperate was London Transport to acquire vehicles which could be put back into working order, at a lesser cost than overhauling DMSs and finish up with a vastly more reliable vehicle, that it snapped them up. RCL2251 is seen here at Barking garage in March 1979, exactly as acquired from London Country, alongside RT2972, both working as trainers.

Instead of consigning the type to a twilight existence on driver-training duties London Transport decided that a number of the RCLs, despite their Green Line fittings, could be put into passenger service and so forty of them were taken into Chiswick works and emerged in the latter part of 1980, with their platform doors removed but retaining their Green Line seats and air suspension, for service at Edmonton and Stamford Hill garages, principally for service on the 149. Here is the transformed RCL2251, representing just about the most comfortable group of buses yet seen in Central London, newly in service at Waterloo.

Following its return to London Transport ownership RCL2221 took on an interesting role, being converted to a cinema bus. It is seen here during an open day at Old Oak Common railway depot in August 1981 with No 92220 *Evening Star*, the last steam locomotive built for British Railways, in 1960, making it five years older than the Routemaster. A Merlin appears to be trying to back into the picture.

There were those who had hoped that, like the 25 SRMs, some RTs might wear silver livery, but this was not to be, and two years later the RT finally ended passenger service with London Transport. The very last route worked by RTs was Barking's 62. RM1256 was one of the Routemasters which finally took over on 7 April 1979, but all eyes – well, practically all – were focused ahead where a cavalcade of RTs, including RT1, its restoration completed only that morning, was about to set off from Barking garage. The semi-detached houses are typical of thousands built between the wars for middle-class families who could aspire to owning a car, although the bus (or tram or trolleybus) would take them to school and work, the car being reserved for weekend outings.

The year 1979 also saw the 150th anniversary of London's first proper bus service, that of George Shillibeer, and one Fleetline and 12 Routemasters wore a most attractive version of Shillibeer livery. RM1191 is seen in Piccadilly.

Another initiative resulted in 16 RMs adorned in a striking bright yellow and red livery operating the 'Shoplinker' network from 7 April 1979, connecting some of the principal hotels and shops in the West End. RM2171 is seen at its Stockwell home. Internally music was played on both decks, interspersed with advertisements in several languages. The fare was 30p, which was hardly excessive, but sadly Shoplinker failed to attract custom away from taxis, and come the autumn the service was no more.

Two London icons for the price of one. Routemasters and a London policeman, complete with helmet, at Oxford Circus in 1980.

The elegant rear ends of Holloway's RM1978 and RM2037 at Aldgate on 19 February 1980. Until 19 years previously one of London's busiest trolleybus termini, this location remains a hive of activity today.

Red remained the colour of the vast majority of London double-deckers, but in the 1970s, on all but the surviving RTs, the traditional London Transport fleetname gave way to the LT roundel. Newly overhauled RM2172 is seen in Vauxhall Bridge Road.

RM1797, working route 52, at Hyde Park Corners, about to be passed by RML2622, minus its radiator badge, on the 74.

10 Scrapping the Routemaster

Twenty-one London Country Routemasters were broken up by Wombwell Diesels early in 1978, but this was merely the prelude, for in 1982 began the scheduled withdrawal of London Transport's Routemaster fleet – not because any of the vehicles were worn out but because they found themselves redundant following a reduction of services in the aftermath of the 'Fares Fair' fiasco. The notion that London Transport would become entirely OPO had been abandoned, so this did not necessarily signal the end of the Routemaster in London, but withdrawal continued apace, and although some Routemasters escaped the scrapyard, either going abroad or into preservation, most were broken up. Contrasting with the situation in the early postwar era, when former London General and LPTB buses were dismantled in the London area, the Routemasters, like the RT family before them, mostly met their end in Yorkshire scrapyards. By the end of the decade around 1,000 Routemasters had been scrapped, but others went on to new careers, either in the UK or, in increasing numbers, overseas.

Meanwhile the future of both Chiswick and Aldenham works, once vital components of a system where the London bus was unique and quite different from that found in the rest of the UK, was now in doubt. In 1985 the two became the responsibility of London Regional Transport Bus Engineering Ltd (BEL) in the hope that they might one day become self-supporting. Amongst the assets were 34 RMAs which had been used for staff transport. The need for such vehicles was much reduced with the run-down of the works, many of the remaining employees using their own private transport, and the surviving RMAs found other roles, including, in a few cases, a return to passenger-carrying duties in Central London.

During London Transport's Golden Jubilee year number of Routemasters appeared in gold, looking quite splendid, whilst others appeared in a close approximation of the original red, white, black and silver colours adopted by London Transport in 1933. The two liveries are seen here adorning RM1983 and RM2116 respectively.

The most appropriate of the specially liveried Routemasters was RM1933, seen here in Trafalgar Square demonstrating what is surely the most handsome livery ever worn by a double-deck bus, with RM623 playing a supporting role. RM1933 would become something of a celebrity and, indeed, remains one to this day, being a regular performer on 'heritage' route 15.

In 1985 staff bus RMA16 was repainted in this dull grey livery; later the window surrounds were brightened up with some red paint, but the overall effect remained deeply uninspiring.

11 Deregulation

On 26 October 1986 bus deregulation took effect throughout mainland Britain outside London, and in some areas free-for-all resulted in fierce competition between operators using a wide variety of vehicles – a situation reminiscent of the 'pirate' days in London in the 1920s and early '30s. Minibuses were much favoured, but at the other extreme it was realised that a double-decker with an open rear platform and a conductor was likely to be the quickest way of clearing the queues and scoring over competitors. But where to find such a vehicle? Manufacture of such had long since ceased, but here was London Transport selling of all its lovely, well-maintained, perfectly roadworthy Routemasters. Perhaps the most remarkable story in the world bus business of the last 25 years has been the success of Stagecoach. Five RMs were bought in January 1985 by this small Scottish firm, run by brother and sister Brian Souter and Ann Gloag, and put to work on local services in Perth and Dundee. From this grew the extraordinary success story of Stagecoach. One of the last functions of Aldenham before its inevitable closure was to repaint

large numbers of RMs in the red and yellow colours of Clydeside. Traditionally the Scots are supposed to be careful where they invest their money (although events in the banking world in 2007/8 might suggest otherwise), and the Routemaster fleet operating in and around Glasgow certainly represented a bargain. Another early user of ex-London Routemasters was Blackpool Transport. The Lancashire resort was long a Mecca for transport enthusiasts, being (until recent years) the last operator of street tramways in the UK. Thirteen RMs, all with Leyland engines, were put to work, adorned in what was basically Blackpool's prewar ornate and rather beautiful fully lined-out red-and-white livery. RM1 just missed the last of the London trams, by two years; it would be another three decades before Routemasters and trams could

Sold in 1988 to Southend Transport, the former RM1183 later passed to London Country. Still in Southend blue and white, it is pictured in 1993 in Kingston-upon-Thames — an appropriate location for a bus allocated when new in 1962 to replace Kingston-area trolleybuses.

be seen working together in the capital, but in Blackpool RMs and trams kept company along the famous promenade.

Meanwhile, although Routemasters were leaving London in great numbers a niche market in the capital which was expanding and which had a use for them was the sightseeing tour. Aldenham did the conversion of 50 RMs in 1985, some to open-toppers, but by now this work and general overhauls could be carried more quickly and cheaply elsewhere, and in 1986 Aldenham closed for good. The last open-top buses built for ordinary service in London dated back to the early 1930s, and by early postwar days such vehicles could be found only in selected seaside resorts. However, the number of overseas visitors to Britain grew enormously with the advent of cheap air travel in the 1960s, and once-grimy cities began to smarten themselves up as the old, heavily polluting Victorian industries died, diesel and electric trains replaced steam, and smokeless zones proliferated. One of the best ways of seeing the sights is from the upper deck of a double-deck bus (a vehicle quite unknown in most parts of the world) and best of all an open-topper. Thus the type began to reappear on the streets of London and other British cities and, despite the unpredictability of the British weather, became very successful, some in London, with the first few rows of seats covered, even managing to find employment all year round.

One of the best ways of seeing the sights of London is from the upper deck of a double-deck bus, preferably an open-topper. The downside to this is the unpredictable English summer weather. Here a group of pupils from Swanage Middle School have, fortunately, come equipped for all eventualities as they enjoy a soaking on a Routemaster in Whitehall in June 1992.

12 Resisting the rivals

Neither the Swift single-decker nor the DMS double-decker had proved itself as far as London Transport was concerned, but a suitable double-decker which could operate without a conductor had to be found, so London Transport engineers got together with British Leyland, and in November 1975 the first prototype, the B15, arrived. Bodied by Park Royal, it bore some resemblance to the DMS, but the most distinguishing feature was the greater depth of the lower-deck windows compared with those on the upper deck. It worked on route 24 and was joined by a second prototype at the end of 1977, by this time the B15 had been officially launched as the Titan. Eventually 1,125 production Titans (Ts) were put into service between 1978 and 1984.

The Titan replaced many Routemasters, particularly in East and South East London, whilst to the north and west another OPO double-decker, the MCW Metrobus (M), also replaced Routemasters, some 1,442 examples taking up work between 1978 and 1986. The vast majority of both types were fitted with the trusty Gardner engine, and both were aimed at provincial operators as well as London

Transport. The Metrobus, similar in profile to the DMS but which had very little LT input, certainly was, but the Titan, designed very much with London in mind, proved too complex and too expensive for provincial tastes, and this lack of interest ultimately resulted in the model's demise in 1984.

Developed as a simpler alternative to the Titan, the Leyland Olympian had been launched in 1980, the first examples joining the London Transport fleet in 1984. No significant alterations were made for use in the capital capital, and only 263 were ordered to London specification, although others would be acquired later. The bus proved popular throughout the UK, but although badged a Leyland it was in many respects a Bristol, having been developed at the Brislington works of Bristol Commercial Vehicles, and most early examples (including the 263 for London) had bodywork by Bristol's traditional partner, ECW.

In the early 1980s, in a bid to increase efficiency and engender local pride, London Transport had organised its bus operations into eight districts (later reduced to six and then five), and in 1988, as a prelude to eventual privatisation, these were

Prototype Leyland Titan BCK 706R on display at the Cobham Bus Museum open day in April 1978.

The first Olympians for London Transport – a trio for comparative trials that also involved Mk 2 Metrobuses, Dennis Dominators and Volvo Ailsas – arrived in 1984 and were followed in 1986/7 by a further 260. Here newly delivered L180 stands inside Norwood garage in 1986, with trainer RMC1467 in the distance.

rearranged to create 11 bus-operating subsidiaries of the recently formed London Buses Ltd. By now more than half the Routemaster fleet had gone, although nearly all the RMLs survived. Those remaining operated 25 routes. Red was still the colour of almost all London double-deckers, Routemasters retaining a white band between the decks, but their condition varied considerably, many being in dire need of overhaul, repaint and tender loving care, although they seldom reached the deplorable state of some RTs in their final years.

The routes worked by Routemasters in April 1989, along with the operating garages and the number of vehicles scheduled for service, were as follows:

2B Norwood (N) 1 RM, 17 RML
3 Camberwell (Q) 15 RM
6 Willesden (AC) 9 RML; Ash Grove (AG) 25 RML
7 Westbourne Park (X) 12 RML
8 Bow (BW) 37 RML
9 Shepherd's Bush (S) 14 RML; Stamford Brook (V) 2 RM, 16 RML
10 Victoria (GM) 2 RM; Holloway (HT) 1 RM, 15 RML
11 Victoria (GM) 29 RM
12 Camberwell (Q) 15 RML; Peckham (PM) 5 RM, 22 RML; Shepherd's Bush 6 RML
13 Finchley (FY) 22 RML
14 Putney (AF) 25 RML
15 Upton Park (U) 47 RML; Westbourne Park (X) 12 RML
19 Victoria (GM) 26 RM
22 Putney (AF) 18 RML
36 Peckham (PM) 25 RM
36A Peckham (PM) 7 RM
36B Peckham (PM) 5 RM; Catford (TL) 18 RM
38 Leyton (T) 40 RML
73 Tottenham (AR) 35 RML
88 Shepherd's Bush (S) 15 RML; Stockwell (SW) 13 RML
137 Streatham (AK) 7 RML; Brixton (BN) 25 RML
159 Streatham (AK) 18 RM; Camberwell (Q) 10 RM, 16 RML
X15 Upton Park (U) 6 RMC

In all 633 Routemasters were scheduled for service, this total comprising 164 RMs, 463 RMLs and six RMCs.

It was recognised that the Routemaster's London career was far from over. Nearly all the Routemasters worked Central London routes which were deemed unsuitable for OPO, and although some parts of most Routemasters would need renewal most were still basically sound.

By the late 1980s almost all of the Leyland-engined examples, being in the minority and therefore considered non-standard, had been withdrawn, but the AEC engines, unsurprisingly, were also showing their age and were in need of replacement. In 1988 RM1894 had been fitted with an Iveco engine, and RM2033 a Cummins unit. Both proved successful, and ultimately more than 500 Routemasters – RMs and RMLs – were re-engined. RMLs were given priority, most of the surviving RMs retaining AEC units, while some of the latter that had been given Iveco engines lost these to RMLs and had their AEC units restored. By the early 1990s, however, it was realised that something more comprehensive was required to enhance the Routemaster's passenger appeal and extend its life expectancy into the 21st century.

Trial refurbishment of RMLs 2648 and 2735 was carried out and presented to the public at Covent Garden in July 1991. This met with general approval, and in December that year contracts were awarded for the refurbishment of 486 RMLs at a total cost of £10 million, which worked out at something over £20,000 per vehicle. So extensive was this work that the completed bus was virtually a new vehicle – which was the description applied to the RT family after each overhaul at Aldenham. RML2360 was the first to be completed, in February 1992, whilst RML895, one of the original Finchley buses and thus 31 years old, was the star of a press launch at the Design Museum beside Tower Bridge, a venue which enabled the assembled photographers to include two London icons in one picture. The refurbished RMLs were splendid and internally a great improvement on the original design with their white ceilings, Transmatic concealed lighting, seats and side panelling fitted with blue, red and grey 'crushed strawberry' moquette. The work was carried out by London Buses subsidiary Leaside Buses at its Enfield garage, South Yorkshire Transport at Rotherham and TBP Holdings at Witton, Birmingham; subsequently a further 16 vehicles were treated by South Yorkshire, bringing to 502 the grand total of buses refurbished, the programme being completed in August 1994.

These latter days of the Routemaster were in complete contrast to those of the RT, apart from being far more drawn out. As the 1970s progressed

In 1991 the decision was taken to extend the lives of the RMLs by embarking on a programme of refurbishment. Here refurbished RML2360 and RM676 wait to return west from Liverpool Street. Since the photograph was taken, in 1992, the terminus of the famous 11 route has been moved to the west side of the rebuilt station, the adjoining Broad Street station having disappeared, the temptation to sell off the valuable land on which it stood having proved irresistible.

Privatisation saw Kentish Bus winning the contract for the 19 route and repainting its RMLs in April 1993 in a livery like nothing any Routemaster employed in ordinary service on a Central London route had ever worn before, as displayed by this one in the Strand.

In 1994 the RMs based at Brixton working the 159 began to appear in an equally startling livery, although there was at least a fair proportion of red. RM719, accompanied by two other Routemasters, one with a distinctly eye-catching advertisement, is seen in Waterloo Place, just below Regent Street, in the summer of 1994.

Metrobus M1035 and a returnee from Scottish exile, RM735, off Oxford Street in 1995.

In this September 1994 picture three RMLs keep company with a Metrobus, a Scania and a National Greenway at Aldgate bus station. Ultimately the Routemaster outlived them all. Nearest the camera is DRM2516, originally RML2516 (JJD 516D), rebuilt in 1991 using the enclosed rear platform from a withdrawn RMC and re-registered with a mark proper to an RM some five years its senior.

the RT had been banished further and further into the suburbs, as indeed, had the STL a generation earlier, although an odd quirk was that the RT, often a fairly scruffy looking one at that, could still be seen at Heathrow, most overseas visitors first sight of London, until July 1978. Still, no doubt many Americans thought them real cute. Throughout the 1990s and, indeed into the 2000s, the Routemaster was as common a sight in the heart of the West End and the City as high fashion, oil sheikhs and overpaid bankers. Above all Oxford Street, most of it restricted to buses and taxis, was the Routemasters' favourite haunt, and hundreds passed up and down every hour throughout the day.

A number of Titans ended their service in London as open-top sightseeing buses, and one is here, operated by the Big Bus Company, being passed in the Aldwych by freshly refurbished RM1204 in September 2001.

13 New owner

Not for the first time the title and status of the controlling body of London's bus services changed, this time at the beginning of the new millennium. The regulatory body was to be London Bus Services Ltd and, not tripping so easily off the tongue, Transport for London would be the overall title, replacing the rather neater, 67-year-old London Transport. The future of the Routemaster, which younger Londoners probably thought also went back that far, seemed to be assured when Mayor Ken Livingstone repeatedly praised it, and with passenger numbers steadily climbing it was announced that RMs, some sold decades earlier, would be bought back, refurbished, and set to work once again on the streets of London. Marshall of Cambridge was given the contract, the first bus arriving in February 2001, followed by another 49. Some had been working in the provinces, some had been preserved, some had even been abroad – and we don't mean Scotland. The most high-profile group, 22 in all, were those which were put to work by Sovereign on route 13, bringing them into the heart of the West End and terminating at the Aldwych; the 13 had long ceased to continue on

The contract to refurbish Routemasters bought back from various of sources was awarded to Marshall of Cambridge. RM1562 stands outside Charing Cross station in the autumn of 2009.

down Fleet Street and through the City to London Bridge. Painted red all over, they could have appeared a rather dull, but such was the shine of their paintwork that the effect was simply dazzling.

In 2002 HM the Queen celebrated her Golden Jubilee, and, as had been the case 25 years earlier, the occasion was marked by repainting a number of Routemasters, 15 of them, as well as an assortment of other types, including RT4712, bringing the total to 50. Modern technology meant that gold vinyl sheets could be applied, which attracted criticism inasmuch as it was said to look drab in certain conditions. Maybe I was just lucky, but every gold Routemaster I saw, whether in rain or shine, looked splendid.

RM1568, another of those reacquired by Transport for London and refurbished by Marshall for use on route 13, heads along Finchley Road on 1 November 2003.

Fifteen Routemasters were among the 50 London buses which in 2002 appeared in gold livery to mark the Queen's Golden Jubilee. RML2648 is seen in Victoria Street.

Celebrity RM6, of Brixton garage, was also adorned in gold, being seen here heading out of Trafalgar Square with a Van-Hool-bodied coach, a red RML and a sightseeing Titan in pursuit.

The end is nigh 14

Despite assurances to the contrary, in the summer of 2002 rumours began circulating to the effect that the Routemaster's days in London were numbered. Technological advances meant that fewer and fewer passengers were buying their tickets on the bus; indeed those that did seemed to be mostly tourists, no visit to London being considered complete without a ride upstairs on a red double-decker. Much more attention was, quite rightly, also being paid to the needs of disabled passengers and to parents with small children in pushchairs and buggies. Even so, a 'new' route, 390, between Archway and Marble Arch, was created in February 2003 and worked by Routemasters, although this was actually the result of route 10, which hitherto linked Hammersmith and Archway, being curtailed and converted to one-person operation.

Another Routemaster route divided in February 2003 was the 36, which henceforth was duplicated for much of its length by the 436 operating between Lewisham and Paddington, the 36 continuing to run between New Cross and Queen's Park. The 436 was worked by that most controversial of vehicles, the articulated Mercedes-Benz Citaro, popularised/vilified in the media as the 'bendi-bus'. Much nonsense was talked about its unsuitability for London conditions and the dangers caused, particularly for cyclists, by its great length. Statistics reveal that these were greatly exaggerated, but it was hardly an ideal vehicle for the narrow streets of the City of London. It also had three doors, two of them unsupervised, and thereby encouraged fare-dodging. Perhaps the greatest opposition came in October 2005, when the type replaced Routemasters on the 38, but when I was in Shaftesbury Avenue a short while later, heading for Victoria with my two-year-old grandson in his buggy, I was able to wheel him straight onto the

RM5 working from Tottenham garage in February 2002. The author travelled on it along Oxford Street and got into conversation with the conductress, who, commenting on the small plaque (on its front bulkhead) recording its unique status as the very first production Routemaster, asked, logically enough, why it hadn't been given the number 1.

The author's wife, Maeve, is surprised to find a cow grazing at Aldwych in the summer of 2002. Painted to represent a Routemaster, it was one of a number of delightfully diverting sculptures unveiled in Central London as part of a campaign to 'keep the capital mooving'. It was sponsored by Go-Ahead.

bus – something I certainly could not have done with a Routemaster.

Possibly the person who suffered most from the replacement of the Routemaster by the bendi-bus was Ken Livingstone. Not only had he reneged on his promise to retain this icon, but his Conservative opponent in London's mayoral elections, Boris Johnson, a past master at courting favourable publicity, despite being prone to regular gaffes, pounced on the supposed evils of the bendi-bus, and this would play no small part in his victory over Mr Livingstone, himself not averse to exploiting a publicity opportunity.

Thus the Routemaster was finally to bow out of ordinary passenger service in London. This did not stop two final commemorative liveries being applied, in 2004. One marked the 150th anniversary of the commencement of the Great Northern Railway's horse-bus service between King's Cross and London Bridge, the other the 175th of George Shillibeer's entry into the London bus business. Both fell well short of the usual standard of special liveries applied to Routemasters and are best forgotten.

At the beginning of 2005 there were just 192 Routemasters still in regular service in London. The last principal Central London thoroughfare to be served exclusively by Routemasters, on routes, 14, 19, and 38, was Shaftesbury Avenue, but this monopoly came to an end on 2 April, when they

The final round of OPO conversions had begun in August 2003, but Routemasters still threatened to outnumber Christmas shoppers in Oxford Street on 13 December.

were taken off the 19. Bendi-buses ousted Routemasters from the 38 on 29 October, and that left just one route, the 159, running from Streatham to Marble Arch. It was fitting that Oxford Street should have been served right to the end, for until a couple or so years earlier the Routemaster has seemed as much a fixture as Selfridges and had had a near-monopoly there.

The penultimate day of normal Routemaster operation in London, Thursday 8 December 2005, saw a remarkable number of London buses, old and very old, appear on the 159. A group of Cobham Bus Museum members, including yours truly, set off for Central London in the oldest bus on view that day, Tilling ST922 – an appropriate choice, for Tilling STs had once operated the 59 group of routes, including the 159, from Croydon garage. One doesn't expect mid-December to be warm, nor was it, especially on a 1930-vintage double-decker, built long before the days of heaters and with an open staircase to boot. But, well wrapped up, we were comfortable enough and made excellent time

The year 2004 marked the 50th anniversary of the Routemaster, and some of the survivors displayed this logo. Route 12 would shortly to be taken over by bendi-buses.

along the A3 and then the Kingston by-pass, where once trolleybuses operated, through Putney and Wandsworth, past St Thomas's Hospital, over Westminster Bridge, along Whitehall, around Trafalgar Square and then back across the river by way of Waterloo Bridge to draw up behind Waterloo station beside the home of bendi-buses and, until a couple of years earlier, the Routemasters that worked route 11.

After a quarter of an hour's pause for the elderly lady to get her breath back, off we went along the 159 route southwards through a remarkably still leafy Kennington, past the Oval – an excellent venue if you are an English cricket supporter and where, in the days of my youth, Surrey, with perhaps the greatest County bowling combination of all time, won the Championship in eight successive seasons. Neville Cardus, that celebrated cricket writer, once made reference to eating one's sandwiches while perched upon on the narrow upper-deck wooden seats of the trams which used to clatter past the Oval, but no such discomfort afflicted any of the patrons of ST922, which, indeed, has rather well-padded, well-sprung seats. On our way through Brixton we passed numerous Routemasters, some in very fancy liveries, not to mention a 'Eurostar' bound for Paris (how *that* would have surprised my father and his colleagues in the NAAFI office in the 1940s!), as well as various RTs, including a Cravens, before turning just short of Brixton garage, which some of us still think of as Telford Avenue, home to the great and glorious 'Felthams'. (How about having a whip-round to bring No 331 down from Crich for a day out on the Tramlink network?) Then it was back to the West End and over Westminster Bridge, where I abandoned ship for a while to join the throngs of photographers, somewhat puzzled-looking office workers, tourists, enthusiasts from far and wide and a taxi-driver who drew up beside me and enquired: 'What's going on?' And I always thought London taxi drivers knew everything – another illusion shattered. A welcome visitor was a lowbridge ECW-bodied green Bristol K of 1949 – TD895 (HLJ 44) – which had expected to begin

Shaftesbury Avenue was the last principal Central London thoroughfare to be served exclusively by Routemasters. RML2685 is seen ahead of another of the type as a third waits to emerge from Charing Cross Road in December 2004.

OPO conversion of the 38 left just one route operated entirely by Routemasters, this being the 159 (Streatham–Marble Arch), worked by Brixton garage. RML892, one of the original batch of 30ft-long buses delivered in 1961, crosses Westminster Bridge in November 2005.

The penultimate day of ordinary Routemaster operation in London, Thursday 8 December 2005, saw a remarkable number of preserved London buses appear on the 159. The oldest of all was Tilling ST922, of 1930 vintage, seen parked alongside gold RM6 of Arriva in Northumberland Avenue. RM6 is a particularly significant member of the Routemaster family, having been the very first production example to be delivered, on 11 May 1959, and in November of that year it was one of the group sent to West Ham garage where it took part in the first replacement of trolleybuses by Routemasters.

its career in genteel Bournemouth with Hants & Dorset but found itself drafted in to fill the gap left by STs, LTs and STLs which, worn out by sterling war work and very little tender loving care during that period, were falling by the wayside in huge numbers. Now preserved by Ensign, it provided a great contrast to several green Routemasters, buses and coaches, also working the 159.

By now owned by Metrobus, RML2317, one of the Country Area buses sent new to Godstone in September 1965, heads across Westminster Bridge on 8 December 2005. RML2317 was returned to London Transport in December 1977, was repainted at Aldenham and served for many years in the West End and City. It was fitted with an Iveco engine in 1991, was refurbished in 1993, had a Scania engine fitted in 2004 and later that year was restored to green livery. In January 2009 it would be sold to fellow Go-Ahead subsidiary Brighton & Hove, subsequently being repainted in the livery of Thomas Tilling, which operator had established a route network in Brighton in 1916. It is now used mainly on tours and private-hire work.

Dusk was falling as I rejoined ST922 in Whitehall. A final surprise was RT624, which drew up alongside. I had last seen it at the Transport Museum, Wythall (on the south-western outskirts of Birmingham), where Malcolm Keeley and friends had graciously allowed it to mingle with Birmingham Corporation Daimlers and Midland Red BMMO D9s (some of which, converted to open-top, had enjoyed an afterlife on the London sightseeing circuit), but as the very last RT in ordinary passenger service it had been authentically restored to its condition of April 1979, when it lived at Barking. The next day Brixton's RMs and RMLs would bring to an end ordinary passenger service for a type which had begun it 46 years earlier.

Another 8 December 2005 picture. The low winter sun dazzles both the driver and the passengers sitting at the front of the upper-deck as RM1 waits at the traffic lights to enter Parliament Square.

RML2573, advertising the heritage routes which will remain after it comes off the road the following day, passes a 21st-century London landmark, the London Eye, as it crosses Westminster Bridge on 8 December 2005.

This was not, however, the end of the Routemaster story in London, for since 14 November two 'heritage' routes, each worked by five RMs, had been operating – a situation that continues today. First CentreWest operates a section of the 9, between the Albert Hall and Aldwych, while East London runs a stretch of the 15 between the Tower of London and Trafalgar Square. Aimed principally at tourists, they also, of course, appeal to enthusiasts. The conductors are obviously hand-picked, their function more that of ambassador and tourist guide than ticket-issuer. It is to be hoped that these routes prove long-lived, but, should they eventually fade away, the Routemaster will surely nevertheless always remain a feature in one form or another of the London scene.

It was decided that a small fleet of Routemasters should remain to operate two 'heritage' services, shortened versions of two long-established Central London routes – the 9 between the Albert Hall and Aldwych and the 15 between the Tower of London and Trafalgar Square. RM324, operated by East London, is pictured at Trafalgar Square.

A 'heritage' Routemaster amongst the traffic in the Strand on 9 December 2006.

Appendix: Routemaster deliveries

	Fleet number	Registration	Engine	Seating	Built	Notes
London Transport						
	RM1	SLT 56	AEC	64 (36/28)	1954	
	RM2	SLT 57	AEC	64 (36/28)	1955	
	RML3	SLT 58	Leyland	64 (36/28)	1956	Weymann bodywork; later RM3
	CRL4	SLT 59	Leyland	57 (32/25)	1957	ECW bodywork; later RMC4
	RM5-300	VLT 5-300	AEC	64 (36/28)	1958-60	
	RM301-631	WLT 301-631	AEC	64 (36/28)	1960/1	
	RM632	WLT 632	Leyland	64 (36/28)	1961	
	RM633-869	WLT 633-869	AEC	64 (36/28)	1961	
	RM870	WLT 870	Leyland	64 (36/28)	1961	
	RM871-879	WLT 871-879	AEC	64 (36/28)	1961	
	RML880-903	WLT 880-903	AEC	72 (40/32)	1961	
	RM904-999	WLT 904-999	AEC	64 (36/28)	1961	
	RM1000	100 BXL	AEC	64 (36/28)	1961	
	RM1001-8	1-8 CLT	AEC	64 (36/28)	1961	
	RM1009	9 CLT	Leyland	64 (36/28)	1961	
	RM1010-1253	10-253 CLT	AEC	64 (36/28)	1961/2	
	RMF1254	254 CLT	AEC	69 (38/31)	1962	forward entrance; sold to Northern General (2145, 3129)
	RM1255-1452	255-452 CLT	Leyland	64 (36/28)	1962/3	
	RMC1453-1520	453-520 CLT	AEC	57 (32/25)	1962	
	RM1521-1600	521-600 CLT	Leyland	64 (36/28)	1963	

	Fleet number	Registration	Engine	Seating	Built	Notes
	RM1601-1719	601-719 DYE	Leyland	64 (36/28)	1963	
	RM1720-1810	720-810 DYE	AEC	64 (36/28)	1963/4	
	RM1811-1865	811-865 DYE	Leyland	64 (36/28)	1964	
	RM1866-1985	ALD 866-985B	Leyland	64 (36/28)	1964	
	RM1986-1999	ALD 986-999B	AEC	64 (36/28)	1964	
	RM2000	ALM 200B	AEC	64 (36/28)	1964	
	RM2001-2105	ALM 1-105B	AEC	64 (36/28)	1964	
	RM2106-2217	CUV 106-217C	AEC	64 (36/28)	1964/5	
	RCL2218-2260	CUV 218-260C	AEC	65 (36/29)	1965	
	RML2261-2363	CUV 261-363C	AEC	72 (40/32)	1965	
	RML2364-2598	JJD 364-598D	AEC	72 (40/32)	1966	
	RML2599-2657	NML 599-657E	AEC	72 (40/32)	1967	
	RML2658-2760	SMK 658-760F	AEC	72 (40/32)	1967/8	
	FRM1	KGY 4D	AEC	72 (41/31)	1966	front entrance, rear engine
British European Airways						
	8208-8232	KGJ 601-625D	AEC	56 (32/24)	1966	forward entrance
	8233-8272	NMY 626-665E	AEC	56 (32/24)	1966/7	forward entrance
Northern General Transport						
	2085-2102	RCN 685-702	Leyland	72 (41/31)	1964	forward entrance; later 3069-3086
	2103	DUP 249B	Leyland	72 (41/31)	1964	forward entrance; later 3087
	2104-7	EUP 404-407B	Leyland	72 (41/31)	1964	forward entrance; later 3088-3091
	2108-2134	FPT 578-604C	Leyland	72 (41/31)	1964/5	forward entrance; later 3092-3118

Chronology

1954	RM1 constructed.
1955	RM2 constructed.
1956	RM1 enters service; Leyland-engined RML3 constructed.
1957	RM2 enters service; Green Line coach CRL4 constructed.
1958	RML3 enters service.
1959	CRL4 enters service.
	Production RMs enter service as part of trolleybus-replacement programme.
1960	RM numbers exceed 1,000 units.
1961	30ft RML class makes service debut with evaluative batch of 24.
1962	Forward-entrance RMF1254 constructed.
	RMC class of Green Line coaches enters service.
	First production Leyland-engined Routemasters enter service.
	New RMs complete trolleybus replacement and now commence RT-family replacement.
1963	RM numbers exceed 2,000 units.
1964	First forward-entrance Routemasters enter service with Northern General.
1965	RCL class of 30ft coaches enters service with Green Line.
	30ft RML becomes standard.
1966	British European Airways orders 50 Routemasters for Heathrow service.
	Rear-engined FRM1 constructed.
1967	Rear-engined FRM1 enters service.
1968	Last Routemasters delivered.
	Reshaping Plan introduces flat-fare OMO.
1969	First all-over advertisement applied to RM1737.
1970	Country Area bus and Green Line coach services pass to London Country.
1972	London Country introduces NBC leaf-green livery.
1975	First RMA-class Routemasters acquired from British Airways.
1976	Spare-parts shortage spawns RT revival on several Routemaster routes.

1977 HM The Queen's Silver Jubilee; 25 'SRM'-class Routemasters painted silver.

1978 Busplan '78 simplifies route network. 'Shoplinker' route operated by specially liveried RMs.

1979 Last RTs withdrawn.
RMC, RCL and RML classes bought back from London Country.
Shillibeer-liveried Routemasters commissioned to celebrate 150 years of London's buses.

1980 London Country's final Routemasters withdrawn.
Northern General's final Routemasters withdrawn.

1981 'Fares Fair' scheme ruled unlawful.

1982 RM withdrawals commence following massive service cuts.

1983 London Transport Golden Jubilee; four 1933-liveried RMs and garage showbuses joined by gold RM1983.

1984 London Regional Transport created.
Last RCLs operate in normal service.

1985 London Buses Ltd created.

1986 Deregulation of local bus services outside London creates new work for Routemasters.
Aldenham overhauls cease.
Original London Transport Sightseeing Tour introduced using open-top Routemasters.

1987 Crew operation reduced to 25% of run-out.

1988 London Buses Ltd establishes 11 bus-operating subsidiaries.

1989 Re-engining of Routemasters with Cummins or Iveco engines commences.

1990 Last Leyland-engined RM operates.
ERM class of open-toppers created by lengthening standard RMs.

1992 London Coaches privatised.
Refurbishment programme commences.
'Central Changes' splits established cross-town Routemaster routes.

1993 Kentish Bus and BTS win first Routemaster-operated contracts using their own liveries.

1994 Privatisation of London Buses subsidiaries.

2000 Greater London Authority created; assumes responsibility for Transport for London.

2001 Marshall-refurbished 'Dartmasters' return to service in London with Sovereign.

2002 HM The Queen's Golden Jubilee spawns 50 gold buses, including 14 Routemasters.

2003 Removal of Routemasters from last 20 routes commences.

2004 'Routemaster 50' commemorates half-centenary of the Routemaster. Operations reduced to 100 vehicles on seven routes.

2005 Heritage routes commissioned (14 November).
Last Routemasters withdrawn from normal service (9 December).

2010 Heritage routes retained by incumbent operators for five more years.

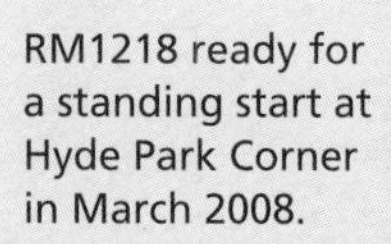
RM1218 ready for a standing start at Hyde Park Corner in March 2008.